THE BERMUDA TRIANGLE

BY MEG GAERTNER

APEX

WWW.APEXEDITIONS.COM

Copyright © 2022 by Apex Editions, Mendota Heights, MN 55120. All rights reserved. No part of this book may be reproduced or utilized in any form or by any means without written permission from the publisher.

Apex is distributed by North Star Editions:
sales@northstareditions.com | 888-417-0195

Produced for Apex by Red Line Editorial.

Photographs ©: Shutterstock Images, cover (airplane and clouds), cover (radar), 1 (airplane and clouds), 1 (radar), 4–5, 6–7, 7, 8–9, 10–11, 14–15, 16–17, 18–19, 20, 21, 22–23, 24, 25, 29; iStockphoto, 13, 26–27

Library of Congress Control Number: 2021915672

ISBN
978-1-63738-160-1 (hardcover)
978-1-63738-196-0 (paperback)
978-1-63738-265-3 (ebook pdf)
978-1-63738-232-5 (hosted ebook)

Printed in the United States of America
Mankato, MN
012022

NOTE TO PARENTS AND EDUCATORS

Apex books are designed to build literacy skills in striving readers. Exciting, high-interest content attracts and holds readers' attention. The text is carefully leveled to allow students to achieve success quickly. Additional features, such as bolded glossary words for difficult terms, help build comprehension.

TABLE OF CONTENTS

CHAPTER 1
LOST IN THE FOG 5

CHAPTER 2
STRANGE STORIES 11

CHAPTER 3
A MURKY HISTORY 17

CHAPTER 4
POSSIBLE CAUSES 23

Comprehension Questions • 28

Glossary • 30

To Learn More • 31

About the Author • 31

Index • 32

CHAPTER 1
LOST IN THE FOG

A ship sails in the ocean near Bermuda. The sun shines. The water is calm. Suddenly, a thick fog rolls in.

Fog makes it very hard for sailors to see or to sense direction.

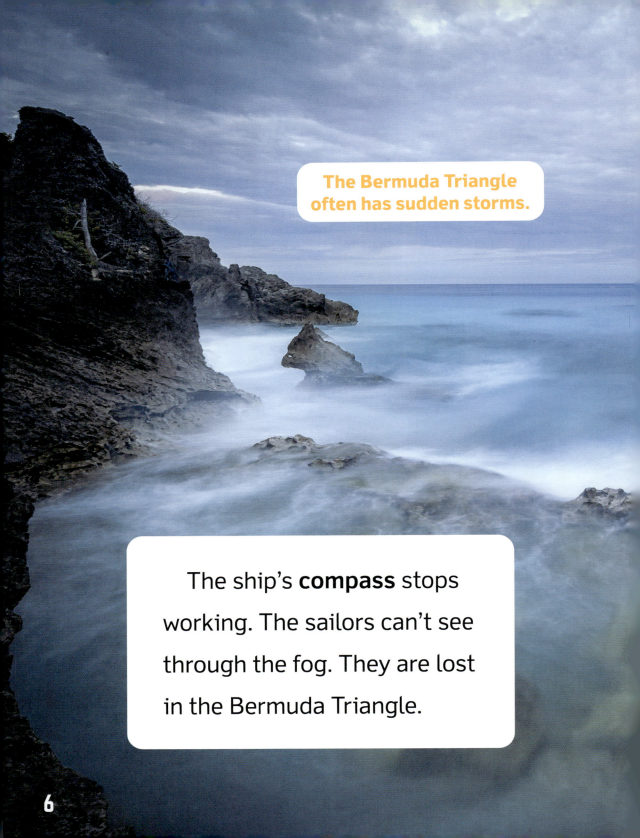

The Bermuda Triangle often has sudden storms.

The ship's **compass** stops working. The sailors can't see through the fog. They are lost in the Bermuda Triangle.

Compasses show directions based on Earth's magnetic poles. But in the Triangle, they sometimes point the wrong way.

A broken compass can cause people to get lost.

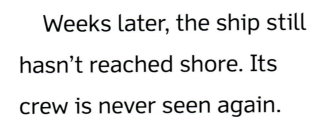

Weeks later, the ship still hasn't reached shore. Its crew is never seen again.

GHOST SHIP

One **legend** tells of a ghost ship in the Triangle. The ship had no crew. Sailors boarded the ship to take its supplies. Fog surrounded them. When it cleared, the sailors had disappeared.

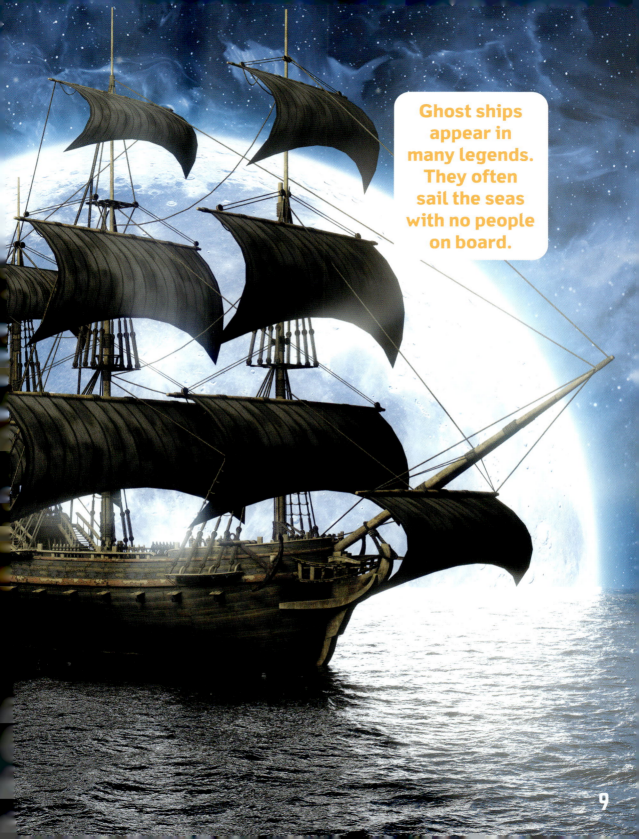

Ghost ships appear in many legends. They often sail the seas with no people on board.

CHAPTER 2
STRANGE STORIES

The Bermuda Triangle is an area in the Atlantic Ocean. It is between Bermuda, Puerto Rico, and Florida.

Bermuda is a chain of islands in the Atlantic Ocean.

Ships and planes sometimes disappear in this area. Often, their remains are never found. Legends try to explain why.

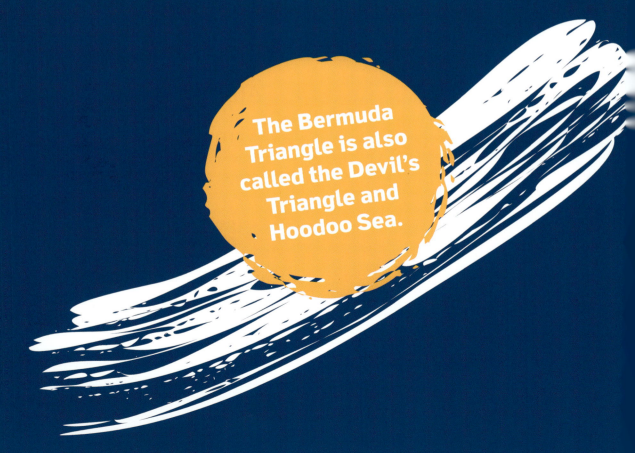

The Bermuda Triangle is also called the Devil's Triangle and Hoodoo Sea.

The Sargasso Sea gets its name from sargassum, a type of seaweed that grows in its water.

SARGASSO SEA

The Triangle includes part of the Sargasso Sea. This sea is a windless stretch of ocean. Sailboats get stuck there. They float among seaweed and **debris**.

Some crews describe seeing strange things before they disappear.

Some legends say monsters eat ships. Others say **aliens** take sailors to study them. Still others say the area leads to another world.

CHAPTER 3
A MURKY HISTORY

Since the mid-1800s, people have reported strange happenings in the Bermuda Triangle. Huge ships have gone missing. So have planes.

People have sailed the waters near Bermuda for hundreds of years.

In 1945, five fighter planes flew near the Triangle. The leader's compasses stopped working. He thought they were flying toward Florida. But they were flying farther out to sea.

The Triangle is blamed for more than 8,000 missing people.

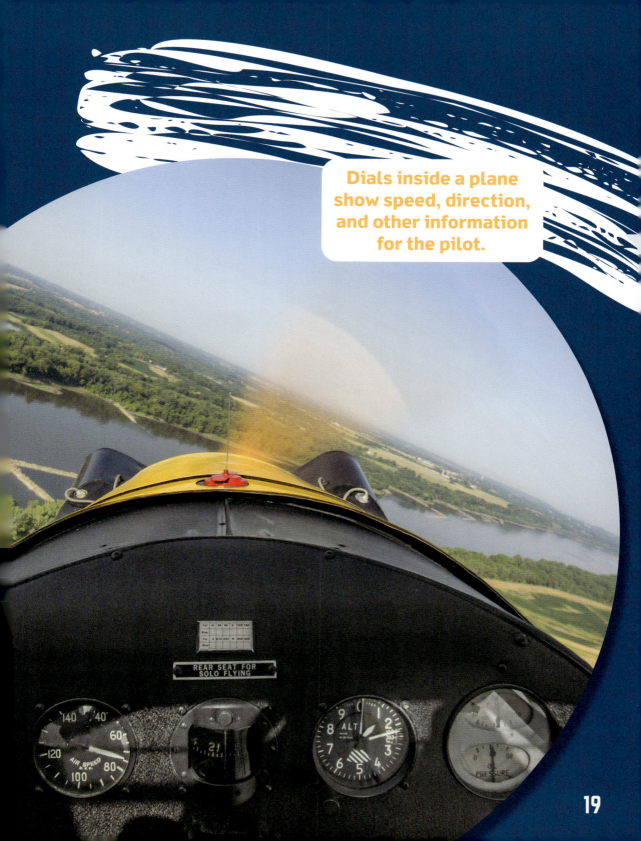

Dials inside a plane show speed, direction, and other information for the pilot.

People on land lost contact with the planes. The planes were never seen again. A second crew went to find them. That crew also went missing.

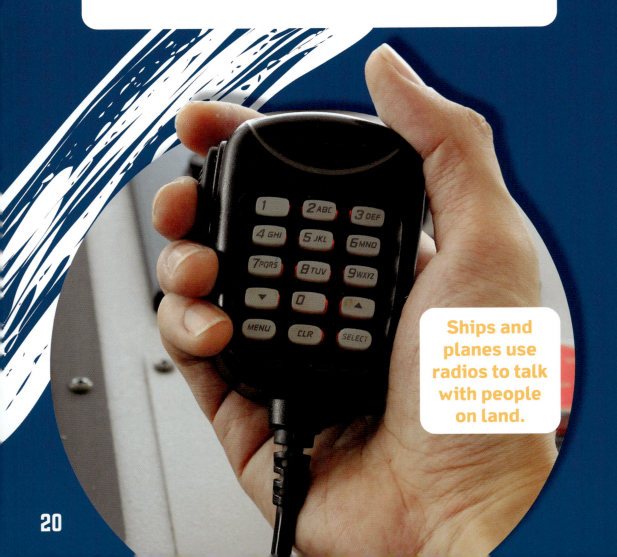

Ships and planes use radios to talk with people on land.

Some planes vanish during storms in the Triangle. Others disappear in good weather.

MISSING SHIP

In 1918, a US Navy ship sailed the Triangle. The ship had **distress signals**. It could have called for help if something went wrong. But the ship never used these tools. It just disappeared.

CHAPTER 4

POSSIBLE CAUSES

The Bermuda Triangle is a large area. Ships often move through it. Most do so without trouble. But some vanish. People aren't sure why.

Despite the strange stories, the Bermuda Triangle remains a main route for ships and planes.

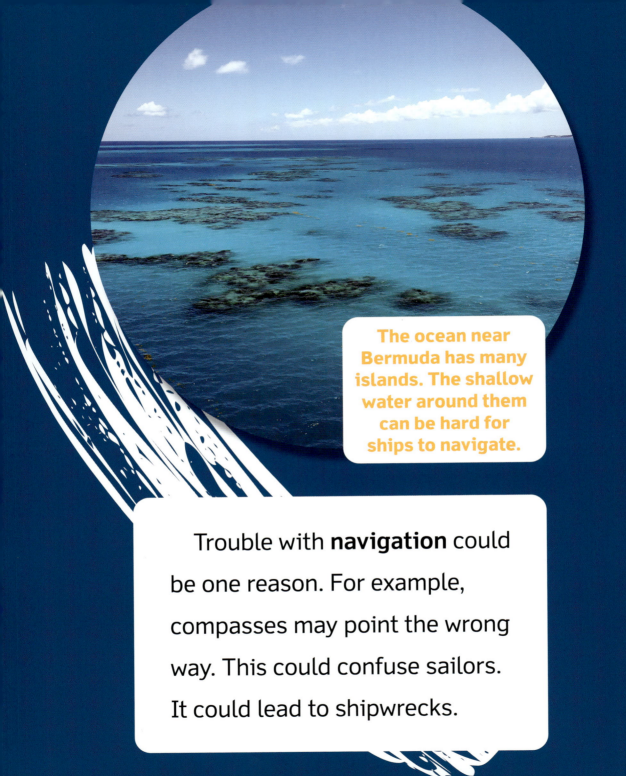

The ocean near Bermuda has many islands. The shallow water around them can be hard for ships to navigate.

Trouble with **navigation** could be one reason. For example, compasses may point the wrong way. This could confuse sailors. It could lead to shipwrecks.

OCEAN FARTS?

Sometimes, the seafloor releases a gas. Bubbles rise to the water's surface. The bubbles could move and sink ships. Also, the gas easily catches fire. If it reached a plane's engine, the plane could explode.

Wrecks of ships and planes are rarely found in the Triangle. But divers do sometimes find them.

In addition, the Triangle has many storms. These storms can cause huge waves. Scientists today can **predict** these storms. But years ago, those storms could have sunk ships.

Some rogue waves can be 100 feet (30 m) high.

Sudden storms can create big waves that can flip or damage ships.

COMPREHENSION QUESTIONS

Write your answers on a separate piece of paper.

1. Write a sentence describing one scientific explanation for disappearances in the Bermuda Triangle.

2. Would you travel through the Bermuda Triangle? Why or why not?

3. When did stories about the Bermuda Triangle begin?
   - A. in the mid-1800s
   - B. in 1918
   - C. in 1945

4. Why could sailboats get stuck in the Sargasso Sea?
   - A. Sea monsters live in that part of the ocean.
   - B. Without sunlight, sailboats cannot float.
   - C. Without wind, sailboats cannot move.

5. What does **stretch** mean in this book?

*The Triangle includes part of the Sargasso Sea. This sea is a windless **stretch** of ocean.*

　A. a movement of the body
　B. an area of land or sea
　C. a hard thing to do

6. What does **contact** mean in this book?

*People on land lost **contact** with the planes. The planes were never seen again.*

　A. the act of touching something
　B. a way to fly in a group
　C. a connection with something

Answer key on page 32.

GLOSSARY

aliens
Creatures that come from planets other than Earth.

compass
A tool with a needle that points north. People use compasses to find directions.

debris
Pieces of something that broke or fell apart.

distress signals
Lights, smoke, or sounds used to call for help.

legend
A famous story, often based on facts but not always completely true.

magnetic poles
The two small areas at the north and south ends of planet Earth.

navigation
The process of finding one's location and planning which way to go.

predict
To say that something will happen in the future.

rogue waves
Huge waves that suddenly rise up in the ocean, sometimes as a result of currents or storms.

TO LEARN MORE

BOOKS
Bowman, Chris. *Flight 19: Lost in the Bermuda Triangle*. Minneapolis: Bellwether Media, 2020.
Orlin, Richard. *Investigating the Bermuda Triangle*. New York: AV2 by Weigl, 2020.
Troupe, Thomas Kingsley. *Searching for Bermuda Triangle Answers*. Mankato, MN: Black Rabbit Books, 2021.

ONLINE RESOURCES
Visit **www.apexeditions.com** to find links and resources related to this title.

ABOUT THE AUTHOR

Meg Gaertner is a children's book editor and writer. She lives in Minneapolis, where she enjoys swing dancing and spending time outside.

INDEX

A
aliens, 15
Atlantic Ocean, 11

B
Bermuda, 5, 11

C
compasses, 6–7, 18, 24

D
disappearances, 8, 12, 15, 18, 20–21, 23
distress signals, 21

F
Florida, 11, 18
fog, 5–6, 8

G
gas, 25

M
monsters, 15

N
navigation, 24

P
planes, 12, 17–18, 20, 25
Puerto Rico, 11

S
sailors, 6, 8, 15, 24
Sargasso Sea, 13
ships, 5–6, 8, 12, 17, 21, 23, 25–26
shipwrecks, 24
storms, 26

W
waves, 26–27

Answer Key:
1. Answers will vary; **2.** Answers will vary; **3.** A; **4.** C; **5.** B; **6.** C